WILDFLOWERS
of the Mid-West

by Greg Keighery

DEPARTMENT OF CONSERVATION AND LAND MANAGEMENT

INTRODUCTION

The Mid-West is one of the most diverse wildflower areas in the world, with a great burst of colour during spring. The northern sandplains is one of two parts of southern Western Australia where species-rich heathlands are best developed (the other is the southern heathlands between the Stirling Range and Cape Arid). Flowering is at its peak in the northern areas in August and September, depending on rains, compared with September to October in the south.

The plants of the northern heathlands, or kwongan, are the typical Australians; the banksia family, the eucalypt family, the boronia family, the southern heaths and the peas. These five families dominate the vegetation types of the region, and provide more than half of the area's species.

In many places, a bewildering variety of different plants coexist in a small area. The region is especially rich in dryandras and there are numerous pea plants, such as the staghorn bush, a daviesia with flattened stems and large nodding scarlet flowers. Low heath dominated by blackboys is common on the lateritic uplands. This plant community is conspicuous around the Badgingarra-Mount Lesueur area. In spring, en masse colour is provided by perennial herbs and shrubs, especially the wattles, smokebushes, banksias, grevilleas, bottlebrushes, numerous species of pea, coneflowers, calytrix and leschenaultia. In late spring, coppercups and featherflowers begin to bloom. One of the most striking featherflowers is orange morrison, which flowers in early summer and can be seen in profusion at Moore River National Park.

This book covers a selection of some of the most common wildflowers that you will encounter when travelling through the Mid-West. It covers an area that extends from Moore River, north of Perth, to Kalbarri and inland to Mullewa.

Above: *Sandplain flora* Below: *Orange morrison*

Photo – Tony Tapper

Photo – Andrew Brown

PLANT RELATIONSHIPS

DICOTYLEDONS (plants with two seed leaves)
- Aizoaceae, the noonflowers — *Carpobrotus* (p.6)
- Asteraceae, the daisies — *Rhodanthe* (p.8)
- Papilionaceae, the peas — *Daviesia* (p.14)
- *Gastrolobium* (p.16)
- Goodeniaceae, the fanflowers — *Lechenaultia* (p.18)
- Mimosaceae, the wattles — *Acacia* (p.24)
- Myrtaceae, the myrtles — *Beaufortia* (p.26)
  - *Calytrix* (p.28)
  - *Chamelaucium* (p.30)
  - *Eremaea* (p.32)
  - *Eucalyptus* (p.34)
  - *Hypocalymma* (p.36)
  - *Melaleuca* (p.38)
  - *Pileanthus* (p.40)
  - *Verticordia* (p.42)
- Proteaceae — *Banksia* (p.52)
  - *Conospermum* (p.56)
  - *Dryandra* (p.58)
  - *Grevillea* (p.60)
  - *Hakea* (p.64)
  - *Xylomelum* (p.66)

MONOCOTYLEDONS (plants with one seed leaf)
- Dasypogonaceae — *Kingia* (p.12)
- Haemodoraceae, the kangaroo paws — *Macropidia* (p.22)
- Orchidaceae, the orchids — *Caladenia* (p.46)
  - *Pyrorchis* (p.48)
  - *Thelymitra* (p.50)
- Xanthorrhoeaceae, the blackboys — *Xanthorrhoea* (p.68)

prostrate shrubs with fleshy leaves and soft white to pink flowers
annuals with heads of soft, papery flowers
shrubs with triangular pods and reddish-orange flowers
poisonous shrubs with sprays of yellow or orange pea flowers
flowers with fan-like petals; needle-like leaves
shrubs or trees with blossoms in fluffy heads
shrubs with brush-like heads of orange, purple or red stamens
star-like flowers with bristle-like appendages
shrubs with white to pink waxy flowers
shrubs with bottlebrush-like flowers on the ends of branches
trees with a conical bud cap, numerous stamens and woody fruits
soft flowers with more than 20 stamens
trees (often paperbarks) with clusters of white to cream flowers
large, soft delicate flowers with hidden anthers
flowers with feathery appendages and less than 20 stamens
woody shrubs or trees; saw-toothed leaves; flowers in spikes
shrubs with dense heads of tubular white, blue or grey flowers
shrubs with heads of yellow flowers and prickly leaves
white, red or yellow flowers in bunches on the stem
woody fruits that split along the upper and lower sides
trees with prickly leaves and woody fruits

green drumstick flowers and a crown of long supple leaves
paw-like densely hairy flowers
flowers have a central lip-like structure with rows of blunt teeth
large fleshy leaves and scented, red or pink flowers
striped similar-shaped petals; flowers in small spikes
spear-like flower-spike; long, tough, hairless leaves

COASTAL PIGFACE
(Carpobrotus virescens)

Family Aizoaceae, the noonflowers

Coastal pigface is a succulent, ground-hugging plant, with attractive pink flowers. Trailing over coastal dunes, this species grows along all sandy and most rocky beaches throughout southern WA. The field of flowers it produces is visited by native bees. The sweet, succulent fruits are eaten by rock parrots and emus, and were eaten fresh or dried by Aboriginal people. Various species of pigface grow throughout southern Africa, Australia and South America, favouring coastal or saline areas. In WA there are seven species, five of them native (two undescribed) and two naturalised aliens.

DESCRIPTION: This prostrate shrub has trailing red to grey branches up to two metres long. The greyish-green leaves are held in opposite pairs and have three faces. These fleshy leaves are up to 65 millimetres long and the pinkish-mauve flowers are 40 to 60 millimetres in diameter and have a white centre. The succulent fruits are a purplish-red colour when mature.

OTHER NAMES: The Aboriginal name is bain.

DISTINCTIVE FEATURES: The species is distinguished from other forms of pigface by its young red branches, and bright pink flowers with a white centre.

HABITAT AND DISTRIBUTION: Coastal pigface grows on the beach or sand dunes from Israelite Bay to Geraldton, including offshore islands.

FLOWERING TIME: Mainly from August to September.

Above: *The flowers* Below: *The fruits*

Photos – Greg Keighery

SPLENDID EVERLASTING

(*Rhodanthe chlorocephalum* subspecies *splendida*)

Family Asteraceae, the daisies

The flowers of splendid everlasting (also known as *Helipterum splendidum*) are among the largest of the everlastings, the spectacular annuals of arid and semi-arid WA. The common name is derived from the stiff petal-like bracts around the edge of the "flower" (actually an inflorescence of small flowers) which are naturally papery and retain their shape if hung upside down to dry. The innermost silky white ray florets have a blackish-purple blotch at the base, which mimics a resting insect and encourages other potential pollinating insects to land on the flowers. In the spring following good winter rains, white "carpets" of this species line roadsides and open areas between scattered shrubs and trees.

DESCRIPTION: This erect hairless annual is densely branched at the base, and has numerous greyish-green linear leaves up to four centimetres long. A 30 to 60 centimetre long stalk bears a single terminal flower head, which is from three to seven centimetres across. The bracts are silky white to pale yellow, while the central florets (small flowers) are yellow.

OTHER NAMES: Silky white everlasting, showy everlasting, showy sunray.

DISTINCTIVE FEATURES: Splendid everlasting is recognised by its large open flower heads and the blackish-purple blotch at the base of the ray florets.

HABITAT AND DISTRIBUTION: This species grows from Geraldton to Minilya, inland to the Gibson and Great Victoria Deserts, and south to Kalgoorlie and Moora. It inhabits a variety of soils, ranging from granite, loam, sandy soils on the edges of saline lakes, acacia shrublands and saltbush habitats.

FLOWERING TIME: July to October.

Photo – Phil Roberts

PINK SUNRAY
(Rhodanthe manglesii)

Family Asteraceae, the daisies

Many species of everlasting grow in arid and semi-arid WA, but pink sunray (previously known as *Helipterum manglesii*) is one of very few found in the wetter parts of the south-west. The unique "bell"-shaped nodding flowers are designed to keep dew and rain away from the pollen. Other everlastings, such as the splendid everlasting, close their flowers overnight, also enclosing any pollinating bees and wasps resting in them.

DESCRIPTION: This erect slender annual has few branches and smooth, hairless, reddish-brown stems. It may reach up to 50 centimetres tall. The leaves are up to four centimetres long and clasped around the stem. Single, bell-shaped flower heads are borne on the ends of long, leafless stems. They are surrounded by overlapping bracts, and are up to five centimetres in diameter. The outer bracts are transparent or purplish, while the inner bracts resemble petals. They are purple at the base and the upper section is pink to deep pink. The tubular flowers are yellow.

OTHER NAMES: Mangle's everlasting.

DISTINCTIVE FEATURES: The nodding flower heads and the smooth broad leaves are distinctive.

HABITAT AND DISTRIBUTION: Pink sunray grows from Kalbarri to Pinjarra, south to the Stirling Range and east to Kalgoorlie and Balladonia. It favours loam, granite, laterite and occasionally sandy soil, and can be seen growing in wandoo, jarrah, jam and sheoak woodlands, mallee, saline flats and herbfields.

FLOWERING TIME: July to November.

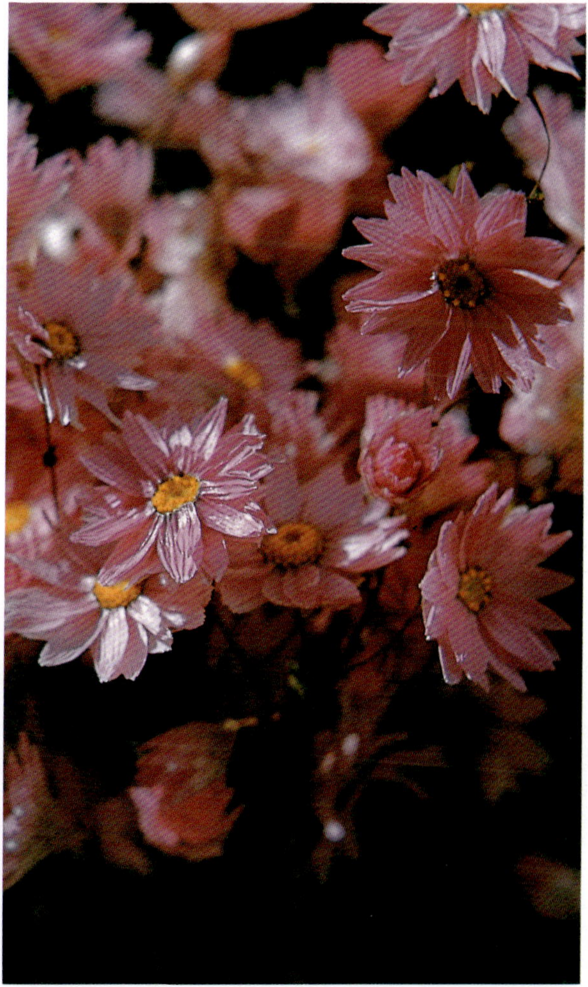

KINGIA
(Kingia australis)

Family Dasypogonaceae

Kingia, which has no close relatives, grows only in WA. Like blackboys, it flowers profusely after fire. Kingia produces aerial roots, from just below the tip of the shoot, which grow down the stem beneath the leaf bases. New ones are produced each year. This strange root system is a reminder that this is a herb masquerading as a tree. However, kingias are very long-lived herbs. Carbon dating has estimated that large plants are from 750 to 900 years old, older than many large forest trees. The common and scientific name honours Phillip Parker King (1791-1831), who mapped much of the north of WA and was the first Australian to reach the rank of Admiral.

DESCRIPTION: Kingia can grow up to eight metres high, with a diameter of up to 40 centimetres. The cylindrical stem is often blackened by fire and covered with tightly packed leaf bases that protect it from fire. The stem is crowned by a mass of flexible green to silky green leaves, up to 90 centimetres long, that hang down when dead. The flower-spikes, or drumsticks, are produced in early spring and take a year to mature. The silky green flowers are narrow, hairy outside and 20 to 30 millimetres long. The fruit is a nut that holds a single seed.

OTHER NAMES: Drumsticks, bullanock.

DISTINCTIVE FEATURES: The green hairy flowers and long flexible hairy leaves of kingia are unique.

HABITAT AND DISTRIBUTION: Kingia grows from near Eneabba south to Bremer Bay in heath, mallee heath or jarrah woodland.

FLOWERING TIME: Mainly from July to September.

Photo – Greg Keighery

STAGHORN BUSH
(*Daviesia epiphylla*)

Family Papilionaceae, the peas

Staghorn bush is one of only two bird-pollinated members of this large genus of peas (the other is the coral pea from near Coorow). Its robust stems provide landing platforms for honeyeaters to probe the very large flowers for nectar. The species flowers in winter when insect activity is often low because of the cold, and frequently wet, days. It also lacks the "eyes", used by bees to guide them to the nectar, which are found at the base of flowers of other daviesias. The scientific name refers to the fact that the flowers are borne on the leaf-like flattened stems. Staghorn bush resprouts after fire.

DESCRIPTION: This low, spreading shrub may reach up to one metre tall by one to two metres wide. The flattened, essentially leafless branches are thick, bluish-green and have triangular lobes that terminate in pointed tips. The leaves are reduced to brown scales. Red flowers are borne in small groups of one to five, with a group of overlapping brown bracts at the base. The petals of the flowers are up to 20 millimetres long.

DISTINCTIVE FEATURES: The flattened, leafless branches distinguish this staghorn bush from all other members of the genus.

HABITAT AND DISTRIBUTION: Staghorn bush grows on lateritic hilltops and in sand over laterite in heath, between Eneabba and the Hill River, south of Jurien Bay. It is most abundant in areas that have been disturbed, such as old gravel pits or roadsides.

FLOWERING TIME: April to August.

Photo – Babs & Bert Wells/CALM

PRICKLY POISON
(Gastrolobium spinosum)

Family Papilionaceae, the peas

This widespread and very variable species has three forms on the northern sandplains. The common form has yellow flowers and relatively soft green leaves. A northern form growing between Northampton and Geraldton has small triangular leaves, while a southern form found from Dandaragan to south of Perth has reddish-yellow flowers and hard green prickly leaves. Like the other 40 species of *Gastrolobium*, this plant is highly toxic to stock and other introduced animals. It produces an alkaloid compound, Monofluoroacetic acid, in the young leaves and buds. This helps to protect these nutritious, nitrogen-fixing plants from grazing animals. All *Gastrolobium* species are confined to southern WA, except for wallflower poison (*G. grandiflorum*), which extends to the Northern Territory. The sodium salt of this compound is 1080, the poison used to control foxes.

DESCRIPTION: Prickly poison is an open, erect shrub that reaches between one and two metres tall. The leaves, which are 10 to 45 millimetres long by 10 to 40 millimetres wide, are in opposite pairs. They are prickly toothed and have a pointed tip. Flowers are grouped into loose clusters. Each flower has a green calyx, up to six millimetres long, and typically has red and yellow petals.

DISTINCTIVE FEATURES: The prickly leaves are the most distinctive feature of this species.

HABITAT AND DISTRIBUTION: Prickly poison is widespread throughout the south-west, from Northampton, inland to east of Kalgoorlie and Widgiemooltha and south to Cape Arid.

FLOWERING TIME: August to November.

Photo – Greg Keighery

HILL RIVER LESCHENAULTIA
(*Lechenaultia hirsuta*)

Family Goodeniaceae, the fanflowers

Nearly all species of leschenaultia are pollinated by native bees, and present their pollen and stigma on a special structure called the "indusium" above the nectary. The fan-shaped lower petals and colours guide the bee under the indusium to pick up or deposit pollen. Hill River leschenaultia lacks these guides, as its large scarlet flowers are pollinated by birds, like those of Burma Road leschenaultia (*Lechenaultia longiloba*). There are 26 species of leschenaultia, and 20 of these grow in WA.

DESCRIPTION: This straggling, prostrate shrub has few branches. It is soft and hairy, with a corky woody base, and reaches up to 50 centimetres high. The narrow leaves, which are scattered along the stem, are 15 to 30 millimetres long, and densely hairy. The scarlet flowers are held in small clusters at the ends of the branches. The petals are 30 to 37 millimetres long and densely hairy inside.

OTHER NAMES: Hairy leschenaultia.

DISTINCTIVE FEATURES: Hill River leschenaultia is the only leschenaultia with hairy stems and flowers.

HABITAT AND DISTRIBUTION: Growing on yellow, grey or lateritic sand, in heath, banksia or mallee heath, this plant is distributed from Zuytdorp National Park to Badgingarra.

FLOWERING TIME: August to October.

Photo – Babs & Bert Wells/CALM

WREATH LESCHENAULTIA
(Lechenaultia macrantha)

Family Goodeniaceae, the fanflowers

Wreath leschenaultia is one of WA's most striking wildflowers. The species grows well in disturbed areas, so it is frequently seen along tracks, road verges, and areas that have been recently burnt. It is, however, relatively short-lived and, unless further disturbance occurs, disappears after a few years. It has the largest flowers of any leschenaultia. The yellow flowers, often suffused with pink or red on the wings, are borne at the ends of the branches. New branches, which radiate from the central rootstock, are produced each year, as the older ones in the centre die off. This maintains the wreath-like habit of the plant.

DESCRIPTION: This ground-hugging plant can grow up to 15 centimetres tall. Its flowers, leaves and branches are hairless. The soft, narrow leaves are 25 to 35 millimetres long, and crowded closely together. The petals are equal in size, but the lower three are spreading, and the upper two are erect. The flowers are 25 to 35 millimetres long, with almost equal, triangular wings, which are five to nine millimetres wide.

DISTINCTIVE FEATURES: This species is easily recognised by its wreath-like habit. The plant dies back to a persistent rootstock in summer.

HABITAT AND DISTRIBUTION: Wreath leschenaultia grows from Nerren Nerren Station inland to Boolardy Station and Wilroy (near Mullewa) and south to Coorow on sand, or sand over laterite, in heath or mallee shrubland.

FLOWERING TIME: August to November.

Photos – Babs & Bert Wells/CALM

21

BLACK KANGAROO PAW
(Macropidia fuliginosa)

Family Haemodoraceae, the kangaroo paws

The black kangaroo paw is long-lived, surviving for up to 30 years. It resprouts after fire, and forms populations of widely spaced plants, unlike the mass display of many short-lived kangaroo paw species. Its flowers are pollinated by birds. The robust stem provides a perch and displays the striking flowers above the surrounding low heath. A few large flowers are presented at a time on each stem, and swing down after maturing to be replaced by a new flower.

DESCRIPTION: This plant has one or more fans of flat, bluish-green leaves, up to 50 centimetres long. Flowers are borne at the ends of branched stems up to a metre tall. Both flowers and stems are covered in black hairs. The green flowers are up to eight centimetres long, with the covering lobes recurved over the back of the flowers.

DISTINCTIVE FEATURES: The black kangaroo paw differs markedly from other kangaroo paws in seed morphology, leaf anatomy, flower shape and colour, and forms its own genus.

HABITAT AND DISTRIBUTION: This species grows on laterite, usually in low heath or mallee shrubland, but southern populations inhabit jarrah woodland. It grows between Walkaway and Muchea.

FLOWERING TIME: Late winter and spring.

Photos – Babs & Bert Wells/CALM

SPOON-LEAVED WATTLE
(Acacia spathulifolia)

Family Mimosaceae, the wattles

Spoon-leaved wattle can turn entire hills gold in winter and early spring, creating an unforgettable sight. It is usually the dominant shrub under illyarrie woodlands in the Eneabba area, where it forms dense stands following mass germination after hot summer fires. Flowering peaks five years after fire. The plants eventually become overgrown by other understorey species and die. Their hard seeds are stored in the soil to await the next fire.

DESCRIPTION: Spoon-leaved wattle is a spreading open shrub, about one to two metres tall by two to three metres wide. The leaf-like phyllodes (modified stems) are thick, fleshy and blunt. They are green and one to two centimetres long. Small round, yellow flower heads are produced in profusion on the ends of the branches.

DISTINCTIVE FEATURES: This species closely resembles some forms of round-leaved wattle (*Acacia leptospermoides*), but can be distinguished by the short, broadly triangular lobes of the calyx and its larger individual flowers, which are fewer and form less compact heads.

HABITAT AND DISTRIBUTION: Spoon-leaved wattle grows on limestones on or near the coast, from Jurien Bay to Exmouth.

FLOWERING TIME: August to September.

Photo - Greg Keighery

Photo – Stephen Hopper

SANDPLAIN BOTTLEBRUSH

(*Beaufortia squarrosa*)

Family Myrtaceae, the myrtles

The comb-like flowers of sandplain bottlebrush bring summer colour to the northern sandplains. Its flowers are predominantly red (especially in southern populations) but may also be yellow, orange, orange with a red base or red with a yellow base. Like other myrtles, such as eucalypts, the stamens have replaced the petals as the attractive part of the flower. The flowers are aggregated into heads, where they function as a single flower. This "brush blossom", as it is known, places pollen very efficiently on feathers, which means a single visit by a pollinator can achieve numerous cross-pollinations. Sandplain bottlebrush is pollinated by birds, so it presents large, brightly-coloured flowers above the foliage.

DESCRIPTION: This spreading or erect shrub has numerous branches. It is one to four metres tall and two to four metres wide. Its small leaves are three to nine millimetres long and two to five millimetres wide. The calyx tube is hairy, and the small, narrow petals are up to five millimetres long. The stamens are 20 to 30 millimetres long and joined for most of their length in groups of three to seven.

DISTINCTIVE FEATURES: Sandplain bottlebrush, unlike swamp bottlebrush (*Beaufortia sparsa*), produces erect inflorescences on the ends of the branches. It also has larger calyx lobes, larger petals and hairy anthers.

HABITAT AND DISTRIBUTION: The species grows on orange, yellow or white sand, often over limestone, in the northern parts of its range, from Kalbarri to Moore River and inland to Tammin. However, it usually inhabits white sand on the edges of swamps, from Gingin to the Whicher Range, south of Busselton.

FLOWERING TIME: The peak flowering period is from December to March. The Whicher Range plants flower from February to March.

Photo – Babs & Bert Wells/CALM

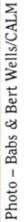

Photo – Andrew Brown

SHORT-LEAVED CALYTRIX
(*Calytrix brevifolia*)

Family Myrtaceae, the myrtles

Bees gather pollen from the flowers of this and most other species of calytrix. They are attracted to the contrasting yellow anthers and pink base of the flower and to the pink petals. After the pollen has been removed by the bee, the basal area turns orange-brown. A bee sees the orange colour as a very dark grey, lacking in contrast, which tells it that no pollen is available from the flower. This relatively long-lived shrub has a single stem at the base and is killed by fire.

DESCRIPTION: Short-leaved calytrix is an erect, spreading shrub, with numerous branches. It is usually less than a metre tall, but can reach up to two metres tall and one metre wide. The thick, blunt and hairless leaves are up to one centimetre long. Flowers are scattered near the ends of the branches. The calyx tube is 12 to 23 millimetres long. The calyx awns are up to 30 millimetres long, much longer than the petals. The pink to magenta petals are yellow at the base and have between 40 and 90 stamens in four rows.

DISTINCTIVE FEATURES: This plant is closely related to short-awned calytrix (*Calytrix truncatifolia*), which grows from Exmouth to Shark Bay, differing largely in the length of the awns on the floral buds.

HABITAT AND DISTRIBUTION: Short-leaved calytrix is found in deep yellow or white sand, often on dunes, in heath or banksia woodland, from Shark Bay to Geraldton and inland to Mullewa.

FLOWERING TIME: August to November.

Photo – Jiri Lochman

GERALDTON WAX

(*Chamelaucium uncinatum*)

Family Myrtaceae, the myrtles

The waxflowers (*Chamelaucium* species) form a uniquely Western Australian genus. Geraldton wax is the best known of the 24 species and is widely cultivated in Australia and overseas. It is probably Australia's most significant cut flower and shows distinct regional variation. For example, a recently discovered prostrate form should produce numerous new varieties when it is incorporated into cultivated plants. Geraldton wax was first collected near the Round House in Fremantle, and local populations can still be found at Bold Park, although the Fremantle populations disappeared in the early 1900s. The species is killed by hot summer fires (bark will protect plants from mild fires), but produces long-lived nuts which lie in the soil and germinate in the following autumn. It has become a weed in New Zealand.

DESCRIPTION: Geraldton wax usually grows as an erect shrub up to six metres high (usually less than three metres), but is occasionally prostrate. The very thin, linear leaves are 15 to 50 millimetres long. The pale pink, occasionally white, waxy flowers are in showy clusters, with separate, spreading petals four to seven millimetres long, that are arranged around a bell-shaped floral tube.

OTHER NAMES: Wax flower, Wembley wax.

DISTINCTIVE FEATURES: The leaves, in opposite pairs, are hooked at the apex and the open, spreading petals of the pink or white flowers are also distinctive.

HABITAT AND DISTRIBUTION: Geraldton wax usually grows near the coast on sand or limestone, from Geraldton to Perth, with isolated inland occurrences around Watheroo and Gingin. Disjunct populations are also found around Kalbarri.

FLOWERING TIME: Cultivated plants flower from winter to late spring, but wild plants flower only from August to November.

Photo – Jiri Lochman

VIOLET EREMAEA
(Eremaea violacea)

Family Myrtaceae, the myrtles

Eremaeas are all beautiful shrubs with well displayed violet or orange flowers tipped with golden stamens. All 16 species are found only in southern WA, and most are confined to the northern sandplains. Like many other members of the myrtle family, such as bottlebrushes, the stamens have replaced the petals as the attractive, colourful parts of the flower. The flowers are often arranged in spikes to increase the visual attractiveness of the plant and ensure pollination.

DESCRIPTION: Violet eremaea is a shrub that grows up to a metre tall, but usually less. It has very spreading branches, which are often almost prostrate. The young branches are hairy, with linear or narrow leaves, seven to 14 millimetres long and a millimetre wide, with a pointed tip. Sweetly fragrant flowers are borne at the ends of branches, usually in clusters of up to seven. They have small, inconspicuous petals and the woody flower base is hairy. About 30 violet stamens, fused at the base, reach up to nine millimetres long. There are two subspecies. One found between Eneabba and the Hill River has needle-like leaves, while a flat-leaved form grows between the Irwin and Greenough Rivers.

DISTINCTIVE FEATURES: The violet flowers distinguish this species from rusty eremaea (*Eremaea acutifolia*) in the north, while the multi-branched lateral shoots and incurved leaves separate it from winged eremaea (*E. alata*) in the south.

HABITAT AND DISTRIBUTION: Violet eremaea grows on deep grey sand and lateritic gravels between Kalbarri and the Hill River, south of Jurien Bay. It only extends as far inland as Eneabba.

FLOWERING TIME: September to October.

Photo – Andrew Brown

ILLYARRIE
(Eucalyptus erythrocorys)

Family Myrtaceae, the myrtles

Flocks of black-cockatoos visit illyarrie when it is in bud, nipping off the inflorescences to feed on wood-boring grubs. The ground below the plants will often be littered with buds. In full flower this spectacular tree attracts large numbers of nectar-feeding birds, as few other plants flower in late summer and autumn. Like sceptre banksia, it helps to bridge the seasons for the resident nectar-feeding birds. The plant produces copious nectar during the evening, so it is available at dawn when bird visitation is at its peak.

DESCRIPTION: Illyarrie grows as a mallee or small tree up to seven metres high. Its smooth bark is pale yellow or white, with loosely attached scattered flakes. The mature leaves are dark glossy green. They are 11 to 18 centimetres long, held in opposite pairs and sickle-shaped. The flowers are in groups of three, with flattened stalks. The large, green, bell-shaped flowers reach five centimetres across, and have a bright red cap, with four prominent lobes. The yellow stamens are in four clusters.

OTHER NAMES: Bokara gum, red cap gum.

DISTINCTIVE FEATURES: Illyarrie is easily recognised by the distinctive square bud cap.

HABITAT AND DISTRIBUTION: The tree grows on coastal limestones, from Tamala Station (south of Shark Bay) to just north of Jurien Bay.

FLOWERING TIME: February to April. Cultivated plants flower from January to May.

USES: This attractive tree is widely grown in gardens and parks throughout Australia.

Photo – Andrew Brown

YELLOW MYRTLE

(Hypocalymma xanthopetalum)

Family Myrtaceae, the myrtles

Yellow myrtle and its close relatives (*Hypocalymma* species) grow only in southern WA. All 21 species are low shrubs with colourful flowers, producing numerous small seeds. Attached to the seed is a small oil-filled stalk that attracts ants, which subsequently collect the seeds and store them in their nests. Seeds taken away and buried by the ants survive, whereas those left beneath the plant are eaten by other insects. Studies have shown that a very diverse range of Lygaeid bugs eat the seeds, which are very nutritious.

DESCRIPTION: This multi-stemmed shrub reaches up to a metre tall and usually has a spreading habit. However, it is occasionally prostrate and, on rare occasions, erect. The old stems are slender and grey, and contrast with the young, hairy stems. The leaves are 10 to 18 millimetres long and three to nine millimetres wide. Yellow myrtle has a profusion of bright to dull yellow flowers, which are very fragrant and have round petals. There are about 60 stamens per flower, and these are as long as the petals, yellow, and joined at the base. The small, brown seeds are attached to a white stalk.

DISTINCTIVE FEATURES: This species has hairless, oblong leaves, which distinguishes it from two other unnamed species on the northern sandplains.

HABITAT AND DISTRIBUTION: Yellow myrtle grows from Geraldton inland to Mullewa and south to Muchea.

FLOWERING TIME: July to October.

USES: Several members of the genus are being developed as cut flowers, and have considerable commercial potential.

Photo – Greg Keighery

LARGE-FLOWERED MELALEUCA
(Melaleuca megacephala)

Family Myrtaceae, the myrtles

As its name suggests, the flowers of this attractive shrub are among the largest of all the melaleucas. The flowers are cream to pale yellow, with gold anthers. This species dominates the low mesas and ranges between Geraldton and Northampton.

DESCRIPTION: This small to medium shrub may grow two metres tall by two metres wide. It has numerous branches and densely hairy stems. The green leaves are hairy when young, and crowded on young stems. The flowers are in large, globular heads, about four to five centimetres across. The tube of the calyx is very hairy. The brown bracts at the base of the flowers are conspicuous when they are in bud.

DISTINCTIVE FEATURES: This species is recognised by its large globular heads of yellow flowers, and by the shape of its leaves.

HABITAT AND DISTRIBUTION: Large-flowered melaleuca grows on sandstone, clay and loam from Kalbarri to Greenough.

FLOWERING TIME: August to October.

USES: This very widely cultivated species is frequently seen in public areas around Perth.

Photo – Greg Keighery

SUMMER COPPERCUPS
(Pileanthus filifolius)

Family Myrtaceae, the myrtles

All five species of coppercups (*Pileanthus* species) are confined to the northern sandplains of WA. Closely related to the Geraldton wax, all species have large spectacular flowers in shades of white, orange, red and pink. Coppercups present their pollen in oil on hairs below or around the stigma. Studies by the WA Museum have shown that a species of bee (*Euryglossa semaphore*) is the sole pollinator of summer coppercups.

DESCRIPTION: Summer coppercups is a slender, erect or spreading shrub up to one metre tall, with numerous branches at the base. The bark is smooth and grey. The linear leaves have prominent oil glands, and vary from eight to 18 millimetres long. Numerous solitary flowers are held in the upper axils, on flower-stalks seven to 20 millimetres long. The tube of the calyx is cup-shaped, covered in silky hairs, greenish-yellow in colour and four to five millimetres long. The soft, magenta to pink petals create a striking display. Each petal is from eight to 12 millimetres long and eight millimetres wide.

DISTINCTIVE FEATURES: The species is recognised by its long flower stalks and magenta to pink flowers.

HABITAT AND DISTRIBUTION: Summer coppercups grows on white or lateritic sand, in heath, mallee heath and banksia woodland, from Geraldton to Gingin and inland to Mingenew.

FLOWERING TIME: December to January.

Photo – Andrew Brown

Photo – Babs & Bert Wells/CALM

41

ORANGE MORRISON
(Verticordia nitens)

Family Myrtaceae, the myrtles

Like the related waxflowers and mountain bells, the pollen of orange morrison is suspended in oil on hairs under or around the stigma in the bud. This species is pollinated by a single species of bee (*Euryglossa morrisonii*), which is partly the same orange colour as the flowers. When female bees lap up the nectar their bodies become smeared with oily pollen. This lovely plant (*Verticordia* literally means "turner of hearts") is very susceptible to dieback disease and many of the southern populations are seriously threatened by this disease.

DESCRIPTION: Orange morrison is an erect shrub up to two metres high. It has numerous slender, erect branches topped with striking golden-orange flowers held in dense clumps. The leaves at the base are up to 60 millimetres long, while the floral leaves are shorter, up to 20 millimetres. The species is killed by fire and forms dense, even-aged stands under banksia woodlands. Its mass flowering in early summer turns the understorey gold.

OTHER NAMES: Morrison featherflower.

DISTINCTIVE FEATURES: Orange morrison is closely related to gold morrison (*Verticordia aurea*), which has larger golden flowers, thicker leaves and flowers earlier in October and November. Gold morrison grows north and south of Eneabba and is also pollinated by one type of bee (*Euryglossa aurea*).

HABITAT AND DISTRIBUTION: This species inhabits grey, white or lateritic sand in banksia woodlands, from Cataby to Harvey.

FLOWERING TIME: November to February.

USES: Once sold door to door around Perth at Christmas, orange morrison was a common cut and dried flower for Christmas decorations before wildflower picking was prohibited. It has considerable potential as a major cut flower crop.

Photo – Michael Morcombe

SCARLET FEATHERFLOWER
(Verticordia grandis)

Family Myrtaceae, the myrtles

Scarlet featherflower displays its large, brightly-coloured flowers above the surrounding heath, with the slender stems providing a landing platform for the birds that pollinate it. Only a few flowers are open on each plant, ensuring a high level of cross-pollination. This shrub may live for a remarkable 50 to 100 years. It produces few seeds, as very few successful germinations are necessary to replace the parent plant over this length of time. Almost all of the 100 species of featherflowers are found in WA, and they contribute greatly to the stunning colour of our sandheaths in spring.

DESCRIPTION: This straggly, spreading shrub may grow one or two metres tall and one to two metres wide. The rounded leaves are greyish-green or green, and nine to 15 millimetres across. Scarlet featherflower is famed for its long spikes of large scarlet flowers up to 25 millimetres across, each with a style up to 25 millimetres long.

DISTINCTIVE FEATURES: This species has rounded leaves, large scarlet flowers and a pair of united bracts which cover the flower when in bud.

HABITAT AND DISTRIBUTION: Scarlet featherflower grows from south-west of Mullewa south to Coorow and near Badgingarra, favouring lateritic sand and sand in heath and banksia woodland.

FLOWERING TIME: It flowers sporadically throughout the year, with a peak from September to December.

USES: It is sometimes grown in gardens and is available from specialist nurseries. It can be grown from cuttings.

Photo – Babs & Bert Wells/CALM

ARROWSMITH SPIDER ORCHID
(Caladenia crebra)

Family Orchidaceae, the orchids

The Arrowsmith spider orchid has evolved a unique strategy to ensure its survival. Like many other spider orchids, it has dull greenish flowers with reddish-purple glands and a movable hinged modified lower petal, known as a labellum or lip. The glands emit chemicals designed to lure male flower wasps. When a male wasp attempts to mate with the insect-like lip, it picks up pollen and transfers it to the next false female wasp. The Arrowsmith spider orchid is one of 40 spider orchids that employ such deception to achieve pollination, but it is the only member of this group on the northern sandplains. The spider orchids (*Caladenia* species) are the largest and most diverse group of Australian orchids, and some 120 of the 160 or so species are found in WA.

DESCRIPTION: This tuberous herb has a single narrow, hairy, linear leaf, up to 25 centimetres long, arising from its base. It produces one or two greenish-yellow flowers on a stalk 25 to 50 centimetres long. The flowers themselves are up to seven centimetres long and up to six centimetres wide. The lip of each flower has a prominent fringe and a central band of densely packed reddish-purple glands, known as calli.

DISTINCTIVE FEATURES: The Arrowsmith spider orchid is identified by its distinctive greenish-yellow flowers, exceptionally dense central band of reddish-purple glands and the long fringes on either side of its lip.

HABITAT AND DISTRIBUTION: The species grows from Dongara to Cervantes, where it usually inhabits sandy soils over limestone. Look beneath a group of illyarrie trees to see if you can find any.

FLOWERING TIME: August to September.

Photo – Andrew Brown

Below: Pollination by a male flower wasp

Photo – Babs & Bert Wells/CALM

RED BEAKS
(Pyrorchis nigricans)

Family Orchidaceae, the orchids

Red beaks is a very unusual, but common, orchid. Colonies of this orchid are usually seen only as large green fleshy leaves, pressed close to the soil surface. However, a summer fire will cause a dramatic change, with most of the plants bursting into flower the following spring. The scientific name refers to the chemical changes that cause the plant to blacken on drying. This is also found in a few other orchids, such as swamp mignonette orchid (*Microtis atrata*). Unlike most other orchids of south-western Australia, the red beaks orchid provides nectar to entice native bees to pollinate the flowers and emits a sweet scent to attract insects to the flowers.

DESCRIPTION: This tuberous herb has a solitary heart-shaped leaf, from two to eight centimetres long and two to six centimetres wide, which lies flat on the ground. From two to six flowers are held on a fleshy, green and red flower stalk, which is around 30 centimetres tall with one or two leaf-like bracts. Floral bracts sheath each flower. The flowers are red striped with white, and the top sepal is prominently hooded.

OTHER NAMES: Elephants ears, elephants tongues, potato orchid.

DISTINCTIVE FEATURES: Red beaks can be distinguished by its large flat fleshy leaf, and fragrant hooded red flowers, attractively striped with white.

HABITAT AND DISTRIBUTION: This widespread orchid grows on a wide variety of soils, extending from the Zuytdorp Cliffs, near Shark Bay, inland to Hyden and south to Israelite Bay. It is also found in New South Wales, the Australian Capital Territory, Victoria, Tasmania and South Australia.

FLOWERING TIME: August to October.

Above: *Whole plant*

Right: *Close-up of flower*

CLEOPATRA'S NEEDLES
(*Thelymitra apiculata*)

Family Orchidaceae, the orchids

Cleopatra's needles, like other sun orchids (*Thelymitra* species), rarely open on cool, cloudy days, but wait until the weather is warm and sunny to display their colourful blooms. Unlike most other native orchids, sun orchids do not have a modified petal known as a lip, or labellum. Instead they have three perfectly formed petals and three sepals, which closely resemble the petals. Cleopatra's needles was first discovered near the Mogumber Mission by students of the Mogumber Primary School in 1965. The flowers of this species closely resemble those of the Star of Bethlehem (*Calectasia cyanea*) and are pollinated by the same small native bees, which mistakenly visit the flowers in search of pollen.

DESCRIPTION: This slender orchid may reach up to 30 centimetres tall. It has a single curved, or occasionally spirally twisted, slender basal leaf and between two and 12 purplish blotched flowers with thin yellow margins. The common name is derived from the needle-like points on the erect, yellow column wings (the ear-like lobes above the central section of the flower).

DISTINCTIVE FEATURES: Cleopatra's needles is closely related to the widespread Queen of Sheba orchid (which grows between Eneabba and Esperance, usually on sandy or clay soils), but has distinctive needle-like points on the column lobes.

HABITAT AND DISTRIBUTION: The species grows on laterite, and shallow sand over laterite, in dense, low heath on hill tops between Mogumber and Eneabba.

FLOWERING TIME: May to July.

Photo – Babs & Bert Wells/CALM

HOOKER'S BANKSIA
(*Banksia hookeriana*)

Family Proteaceae

Flowering between April and October, Hooker's banksia usually dominates the low heathlands in which it is found. Because it is killed by fire and subsequently regenerates from seed, it tends to grow in dense, even-aged stands. This beautiful banksia is a major food source for honeyeaters and honey possums. Though it is extensively harvested as a cut flower, it is not widely grown. As harvesting in the wild may affect the long term survival of this restricted species, a management plan has been formed to encourage the production of flowers from farmed plants.

DESCRIPTION: Hooker's banksia is a dense rounded shrub, growing up to three metres tall by three metres wide, and branching near the base. The young branches are covered with dense hair. The narrow, dull green leaves are up to 25 centimetres long, and have teeth dividing the leaf to near the middle. The cylindrical flower-spikes are up to 10 centimetres long, pinkish-grey in bud, and orange when open. Each spike carries hundreds of flowers, with the buds on the top opening first. The difference in colour between the open flowers and buds gives it the appearance of a large acorn. The fruiting spikes retain the persistent remains of the flowers.

DISTINCTIVE FEATURES: The short inflorescence and slender, toothed leaves of Hooker's banksia distinguish it from other grey to orange-flowered banksias of the northern sandplains. Burdett's banksia (*B. burdettii*) is similar but flowers in summer. Unlike woolly orange banksia (*B. victoriae*) and acorn banksia (*B. prionotes*) it never forms a tree, although natural hybrids between Hooker's banksia and acorn banksia are found near Lake Indoon.

HABITAT AND DISTRIBUTION: Hooker's banksia grows in deep yellow or white sand within heath, from Arrowsmith Lake to Eneabba. It usually dominates the vegetation of this area.

FLOWERING TIME: April and October.

Photos – Tony Tapper

SCEPTRE BANKSIA
(Banksia sceptrum)

Family Proteaceae

This summer flowering banksia provides a spectacular display in the intense heat, when few tourists are abroad to witness it. However, it is a major food source for the local honeyeaters, insects and honey possums, providing nectar in the lean period between spring and autumn, when few banksias or eucalypts are in flower. The plant was named sceptre banksia because the style of the flower has a distinct "S" bend in the upper third.

DESCRIPTION: Sceptre banksia forms a tall spreading shrub, reaching up to five metres tall by four metres wide, and branching from near the base. It has short oblong, dull greyish-green leaves up to 80 millimetres long. These are bordered by small teeth and appear to be cut off at the end. Large yellow flower-spikes, up to 20 centimetres long, are held above the leaves. The fruits are covered by the persistent remains of the old flowers.

DISTINCTIVE FEATURES: No other banksia has a style with an S bend. The flower-spike is at the end of the branch. Initially felty brown in colour, it takes between six and seven months to develop, the longest for any banksia.

HABITAT AND DISTRIBUTION: Sceptre banksia grows on deep yellow or red sands, often on dunes, from Shark Bay to Geraldton and inland to Mullewa.

FLOWERING TIME: December to January.

USES: Sceptre banksia has been planted along the freeways around Perth, where it provides a spectacular summer display, without being watered.

Photo – Babs & Bert Wells/CALM

PLUME SMOKEBUSH
(Conospermum incurvum)

Family Proteaceae

Growing in dense stands several years after fire, these relatively short-lived plants produce masses of fluffy white to pale grey flowers. The flowers are held above the plant, and give the illusion of drifting smoke as they move in the breeze. Plume smokebush is found only in WA, although the genus extends to eastern Australia. When insects probe smokebush flowers, the style snaps down across the tube, daubing the visitor with an adhesive. The anthers explode and shoot pollen onto the visitor, which then transfers pollen to another flower. Several varieties of conospermum bees (*Leioproctus* species) only visit smokebushes. The male bees have a dense covering of white hairs, have white eyes and milky wings and are almost impossible to detect when they lie in wait for females on the flowers.

DESCRIPTION: Plume smokebush is a low, densely branched shrub up to one metre tall. Linear leaves, up to three centimetres long, are crowded onto the lower half of the branches. The leaves are incurved (hence the specific name). Leafless, arching flower stalks may stretch up to 60 centimetres above the foliage and bear two to four bunches of flowers. The white to pale grey, silky flowers are tubular, reddish-purple inside and up to two centimetres long.

DISTINCTIVE FEATURES: The long, leafless flower stalk and incurved, needle-like leaves distinguish this species from the closely related one-sided smokebush (*Conospermum unilaterale*), which also grows on the northern sandplains.

HABITAT AND DISTRIBUTION: Plume smokebush can be seen between Pinjarra and Carnamah, growing in heath or banksia woodlands. It inhabits sandy soils, often with laterite.

FLOWERING TIME: July to November.

Photo – Andrew Brown

SHAGGY DRYANDRA

(Dryandra speciosa)

Family Proteaceae

Dryandras grow only in southern WA. Most of the 92 species of dryandra are pollinated by nectar-feeding birds and display their flowers high up on the branches, with the styles curving into the centre to place pollen on facial feathers. Shaggy dryandra hides its flowers under the bush, holding all the flowers in bud until they suddenly open when probed by the snout of a honey possum from beneath. This places a large load of pollen on the animal so that many flowers may be pollinated in one visit by a honey possum.

DESCRIPTION: Shaggy dryandra grows as a low, spreading rounded shrub up to one metre tall by a metre wide. The margins of its narrow, linear, dull green leaves are rolled under. The pendulous flower heads are borne on the old wood and tend to be under the plant, often close to the ground. The heads are up to seven centimetres in diameter. They are surrounded by circles of feathery, greyish-brown bracts up to five centimetres long, with the outer ones curving away from the head. Flowers vary in colour from yellow to reddish-brown. Flower heads retained on the bush after flowering will turn grey and give the plant a shaggy appearance.

DISTINCTIVE FEATURES: The nodding flower heads, which resemble a miniature protea, are unique. This species and awl-leafed honeypot (*D. subulata*) are the only dryandras without teeth on their leaves.

HABITAT AND DISTRIBUTION: There are two subspecies of shaggy dryandra. One grows on sandy clay in the Wheatbelt, between Narembeen and Tammin, and has more flowers and smaller fruits in the head. The other is found on lateritic sand between Tathra National Park and Badgingarra.

FLOWERING TIME: Usually May to July, but sometimes flowers as late as September.

Photo – Greg Keighery

FLAME GREVILLEA
(*Grevillea eriostachya*)

Family Proteaceae

Flame grevillea bears bright orange flowers, with a light honey scent, in toothbrush-shaped inflorescences. These are presented parallel to the ground, on tall floral branches above the plant, and provide an ideal perch for the honeyeaters that pollinate this species. The parallel flowers also ensure that the copious nectar does not drip out. Some populations of flame grevillea respond to fire by resprouting, while others are killed by fire and reseed.

DESCRIPTION: Flame grevillea is an open or spreading shrub with few branches, that reaches up to two metres tall and two metres wide. The floral branches can be up to three metres above the foliage. The greyish-green leaves are from five to 30 centimetres long. They are usually undivided but may have two to seven lobes. The toothbrush-shaped inflorescences are borne in groups of two to seven on the ends of the floral branches and are seven to 20 centimetres long. Flowers are green in bud and yellowish-orange when open.

OTHER NAMES: Orange grevillea, desert grevillea, yillyiralba and kaliny-kalinypa in the Central Desert.

DISTINCTIVE FEATURES: Flame grevillea is closely related to the tree flame grevillea (*Grevillea excelsior*), which grows on sandplains in the Wheatbelt and western Goldfields. Tree flame grevillea is a tree with bright orange flowers and no emergent floral branches.

HABITAT AND DISTRIBUTION: Growing on deep red, yellow or white sand, flame grevillea is very widespread, extending from near Gingin, through the northern sandplains and the Pilbara to Derby. It is also found in inland deserts to the Northern Territory and northern South Australia.

FLOWERING TIME: Flame grevillea can be found in flower at any time of the year, depending on rainfall in the desert regions, but usually flowers in spring on the northern sandplains.

USES: In the desert, Aboriginal people used the flowers either directly or steeped in water as a drink.

OLD SOCKS
(Grevillea leucopteris)

Family Proteaceae

Old socks dominates the heathlands around Kalbarri by sight and smell when flowering in late spring. Its tall, arching floral branches terminate with masses of white flowers. The sickly-sweet scent dominates the warm still nights, attracting moths and honey possums to the flowers. It is a spectacular shrub for parks and road verges, but its overpowering aroma means it is best enjoyed from a distance. It is, however, an aggressive coloniser, growing very quickly from seed (as it is killed by fire in its native habitat). This species has become a weed in Perth and should not be planted near bushland.

DESCRIPTION: This large, rounded shrub will reach three metres tall and three metres wide, with floral branches arching three metres above the foliage. The leaves, up to 35 centimetres long, have numerous lobes. The pink floral bracts are large, sticky and glandular and, with the pink buds, develop months before the flowers. Several bunches of inflorescences, on the end of each floral branch, bear numerous white flowers.

OTHER NAMES: White plume grevillea, plume grevillea.

DISTINCTIVE FEATURES: The tall arching floral branches and relatively soft leaves distinguish this species from other grevilleas.

HABITAT AND DISTRIBUTION: Old socks grows in deep yellow or white sand, often over limestone, from Kalbarri to Marchagee.

FLOWERING TIME: October to November.

Photo – Stephen Hopper

NEEDLES AND CORKS
(Hakea obliqua)

Family Proteaceae

Needles and corks is killed by fire and retains the woody, corky fruits on the plant between fires. The fruits open after the plant dies, releasing the winged seeds into the cool ash and soil. It is one of several species of hakea that grows in the sandplains north of Perth and east of Albany, but not in between. Cauliflower hakea (*Hakea corymbosa*), ashy-leaved hakea (*H. cinerea*) and fan-leaved hakea (*H. flabellifolia*) have similar distributions.

DESCRIPTION: This erect shrub produces dense branches from near its base and produces slender flowering branches up to three metres high. Its leaves are rigid, circular in cross-section and up to five centimetres long, with a pointed tip. The flowers are in stalkless clusters of between eight and 15. The white outer floral whorl is slightly hairy, up to seven millimetres long, and has a long red style. The mature fruit, four centimetres long and 25 millimetres wide, tapers to a beak and is covered with rough, corky bark.

DISTINCTIVE FEATURES: This species differs from the closely related Brook's hakea (*Hakea brooksiana*), which has fruit covered with thick corky outgrowths and yellowish-green flowers.

HABITAT AND DISTRIBUTION: Needles and corks inhabits the northern sandplains from Yuna to near Gingin and the southern sandplains from the Stirling Range to Israelite Bay. It grows in areas of mallee and banksia heath, in sand or sand over laterite.

FLOWERING TIME: September to October.

Photo – Ernst Wittwer/Wildflower Society Collection

SANDPLAIN WOODY PEAR

(Xylomelum angustifolium)

Family Proteaceae

Sandplain woody pear is usually a tall, multi-stemmed shrub or small tree up to seven metres high, capable of resprouting after fires. Its distinctive pear-shaped woody fruits form a very attractive and ornamental feature of the plant. Only a few of the flowers at the base of the inflorescence have functioning ovaries, and can form fruits. The rest act as male flowers, providing more pollen and nectar to visiting bees and wasps and increasing the size and attractiveness of the inflorescence. Each inflorescence, though made up of numerous individual flowers, actually functions as a single flower, and can only support a single fruit.

DESCRIPTION: The bark of sandplain woody pear is smooth and grey. It has linear leaves, up to 15 centimetres long. They have no teeth but end in a rigid point. Pure white flowers are borne in dense spikes up to 10 centimetres long. The outer floral whorl is hairy and about seven millimetres long. The large, light grey fruit is covered in short greyish hairs.

DISTINCTIVE FEATURES: The multi-stemmed habit and toothless linear leaves of sandplain woody pear distinguish it from other species of woody pear.

HABITAT AND DISTRIBUTION: Sandplain woody pear grows in heath, where it is generally the largest plant. It prefers sand, or sand over laterite, and ranges from Cooloomia (north of Kalbarri), east to Wyalkatchem and south to Corrigin and Kulin.

FLOWERING TIME: December to January.

The fruits

Photos – Greg Keighery

SPIKY GRASSTREE
(Xanthorrhoea acanthostachya)

Family Xanthorrhoeaceae

These long-lived tree-like relatives of the lilies are among the most striking and characteristic plants in southern Australia. There are 28 species of grasstree, commonly known as blackboys. All are confined to Australia, and nine species are found in WA. All are very fire resistant, and usually flower en masse in the year after a fire. The tall flowering spikes are then very noticeable above the burnt vegetation. The strongly-scented flowers of spiky grasstree are rich in nectar and attract a wide range of insect, bird and mammal pollinators.

DESCRIPTION: Spiky grasstree has a short trunk up to one and a half metres high, with one or rarely two crowns. The stem is unbranched and is formed from the old leaf bases. Numerous greyish-green leaves form a hemispherical crown. The thin leaves reach up to 70 centimetres long and end in a pointed tip. The flower-spike, between 50 centimetres and one metre long, is purplish-green or green. The flowers are white.

DISTINCTIVE FEATURES: The short stem, relatively short leaves and prickly flower-spike distinguish this species from other grasstrees. There are, however, two distinctive forms. The northern form has a purplish-green spike, hairy petals, and large pointed bracts at the base of the inflorescence, whereas the southern form displays a green spike and very prominent pointed bracts.

HABITAT AND DISTRIBUTION: Spiky grasstree grows well in laterites in the northern part of its range and on yellow colluvial sands around Perth. It extends from Eneabba to Perth. The southern form occurs only on the foothills and Darling escarpment between Muchea and Dardanup.

FLOWERING TIME: August to November.

Photo – Greg Keighery

SIGHTING RECORD

SPECIES	REMARKS
coastal pigface	
splendid everlasting	
pink sunray	
kingia	
staghorn bush	
prickly poison	
Hill River leschenaultia	
wreath leschenaultia	
black kangaroo paw	
spoon-leaved wattle	
sandplain bottlebrush	
short-leaved calytrix	
Geraldton wax	
violet eremaea	
illyarrie	
large-flowered melaleuca	

SIGHTING RECORD

SPECIES	REMARKS
summer coppercups	
orange morrison	
scarlet featherflower	
Arrowsmith spider orchid	
red beaks	
Cleopatra's needles	
Hooker's banksia	
sceptre banksia	
plume smokebush	
shaggy dryandra	
flame grevillea	
old socks	
needles and corks	
sandplain woody pear	
spiky grasstree	

Photos – Babs & Bert Wells/CALM

INDEX

Arrowsmith spider orchid	46-47	orange morrison	42-43
banksias	52-55	orchids	46-51
black kangaroo paw	22-23	pigface	6-7
bottlebrushes	26-27	pink sunray	10-11
calytrix	28-29	plume smokebush	56-57
Cleopatra's needles	50-51	prickly poison	16-17
coastal pigface	6-7	red beaks	48-49
coppercups	40-41	sandplain bottlebrush	26-27
dryandras	58-59	sandplain woody pear	66-67
everlastings	8-11	scarlet featherflower	44-45
featherflowers	42-45	sceptre banksia	54-55
flame grevillea	60-61	shaggy dryandra	58-59
Geraldton wax	30-31	short-leaved calytrix	28-29
grasstree	68-69	smokebush	56-57
grevilleas	60-63	spider orchids	46-47
hakeas	64-65	spiky grasstree	68-69
Hooker's banksia	52-53	splendid everlasting	8-9
Hill River leschenaultia	18-19	spoon-leaved wattle	24-25
illyarrie	34-35	staghorn bush	14-15
kangaroo paws	22-23	summer coppercups	40-41
kingia	12-13	verticordias	42-45
large-flowered melaleuca	38-39	violet eremaea	32-33
leschenaultias	18-21	wattles	24-25
melaleucas	38-39	woody pear	66-67
needles and corks	64-65	wreath leschenaultia	20-21
old socks	62-63	yellow myrtle	36-37